fair start

an observation of
Possilpark Befriending Project

Save the Children

Registered Charity No. 213890

Argyll
publishing

© Argyll Publishing & Save the Children

First published 1994
Argyll Publishing
Glendaruel
Argyll PA22 3AE
Scotland

© Photos Jenny Mathews
Photographs do not represent the young people
interviewed.

**British Library Cataloguing-in-Publication Data.
A catalogue record for this book is available from
the British Library.**

ISBN 1 874640 26 2

Typeset and origination
Cordfall Ltd, Glasgow

Printing
Martins the Printers, Berwick upon Tweed

fair start—
under 5s at St Mathew's playgroup,
Possilpark

metal gate, Byshot Street

Foreword

Save the Children is an international children's charity committed to making a reality of children's rights. Work is carried out in the United Kingdom as well as abroad to secure lasting benefits to children in a changing world.

In 1994 Save the Children is celebrating its 75th anniversary. The 1990s have brought fresh challenges to the organisation. There are around 100 projects in the UK. These are concentrated in areas where poverty, bad housing, discrimination and abysmal job prospects all conspire to prevent children getting the start in life they deserve.

But what start in life do our children deserve?

The UN Convention on the Rights of the Child sets minimum standards for the treatment of children. Children deserve, and by statute now have the right to, adequate services, protection from abuse, participation in decisions which affect them, and a voice to express their views.

Yet statistics show that poverty affecting children, families and young people has increased over the last few years and that poverty equates with not having a voice, disempowerment and feelings of worthlessness. There is therefore a long way to go before children's rights become a reality in the UK.

The Possilpark Befriending Project staff recruit train and support adult volunteers who give their time to befriend children and young people aged 8 to 18. Since 1986, project staff have matched over 200 youngsters with volunteers drawn from throughout Glasgow. The success the project has achieved hasn't come without careful monitoring and a considered input into the lives of the young people and their families.

This report is being published because it not only establishes the usefulness of befriending vulnerable children and young people, but highlights the obstacles to a fair start for many of our children.

In the following pages we have given the young people we have worked with a voice to express themselves to a wider audience. I hope you find their views of interest.

Brian Wright
Project Leader
Possilpark Befriending Project
42 Allander Street
Glasgow G22 5HD

041 336 2439

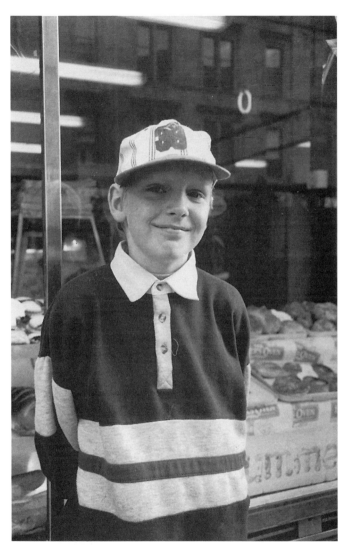

fair start—
outside a shop in Saracen Street

Possilpark Befriending
&
Befriending Plus Project

The Possilpark Befriending and Befriending Plus Project, managed by Save the Children, is located in an area of North East Glasgow where young people experience a lack of choice, resources and developmental opportunities.

The Project aims to provide disadvantaged, vulnerable children and young people with a supportive and challenging relationship with a caring adult.

We aim to provide a quality service by working in partnership with children and young people, Strathclyde Regional Council Social Work Department and other agencies.

Our work is based on a knowledge of and commitment to the Rights of the Child as stated in the UN Convention.

Project aims

Introduction

The Possilpark Befriending Project was set up in August 1986 by Save the Children Fund in partnership with Strathclyde Regional Council. Its aim was to offer certain children and young people the advantages of a stable friendship with an adult volunteer.

The approach is based on the idea that support in their local community is what's needed by many youngsters who are having problems at home, at school or in the neighbourhood. Taking part in the scheme is by voluntary agreement on the young person's side too.

What follows was commissioned as an independent piece of observation with a remit to establish whether the investment in befriending has had any lasting consequences on the young people who have participated in the project over the last 6 years.

Independent observation, like independent consultants reports, it is fair to say, have fallen somewhat in public estimation. This 'independent observer' for one, has doubts about the concept. The truth is that none of us are truly 'independent'. We all come in with a set of pre-conceptions.

In November 1993 when I did the work for this, emanating from government social policy measures, there had been months of mass media coverage about young people, criminality, single parents, personal morality and how parents should bring up children. So issues which instantly arise in places like Glasgow's Possilpark—poverty and feelings of lack of participation in the political process—are already hot.

The author's personal starting point in these things could be typified by several things—my own childhood years growing up in public housing in central Scotland; my own work experience with children and families where the connections between what people can make of their lives and what chances they get seem almost blindingly clear; and a belief in human capacity always to interpret and act on our world. Shooting up heroin, or taking and driving away a nice car are at root a response—often destructive, sometimes tragic, usually ill-considered—to the problem we all have as individuals in making sense of our external world.

Young people's names and some details have been changed to preserve anonymity.

Derek Rodger, Argyll Publishing
February 1994

Fair Start

The flats on the stair at 42 Allander Street, in the inter-war Keppoch council housing scheme in Glasgow's Possilpark, are truly exceptional. The whole stair is turned over to office accommodation. But what really marks them out from their neighbours on the block is not just that they do not actually house families, but that the flats at No 42 all have central heating.

I go through ground floor reception and security door up to the top 3-apartment which is home, not to a family of four, but to the Possilpark Befriending Scheme. In these quarters, two bedrooms and a living room, the office space is intimate. On this sharp November morning, the central heating is belting it out—the radiator can't be touched—and one sash window is open in the workroom shared by project leader Brian Wright and his colleague Charlie Barker.

But in this well-heated and adequately ventilated room the blutack holding the Save the Children Fund

RIGHT TO A FAIR START poster is losing the battle. The poster, which declares a child's right to quality education, health care and housing, is squint over a crack in the chimney breast. The omnipresent damp is doing its work.

The housing blocks that are the parallel Allander, Stoneyhurst and Killearn Streets were never fitted with central heating. It's fair to assume few of the tenants have ever had such a necessity installed. Accusations by housing officials and other experts of improper heating and ventilation as the cause of incipient dampness are legion and now, in the whole of the West of Scotland's public housing stock, folkloric.

The housing blocks in the Keppoch scheme don't exactly inspire confidence. They look damp, even on a dry sunny day, on the outside. These three streets off the main Saracen Street thoroughfare invite all the clichés now routinely attached to much of Scotland's municipal housing stock. The facts are there is an absence of parked cars, a profusion of litter, hardly a soul about in mid-morning and most of Killearn Street's windows are boarded up. Much of this scheme, one of many put up in Glasgow's long and fractious housing history to clear city slums, is now due for demolition. It looks like an area housing a population that has been ground into submission.

Charlie Barker is halfway through the sentence as she bustles into the room where Brian Wright, in response to my questioning, is digging out facts and figures about the project.

"These girls' magazines," she is saying, "I haven't read them for years . . . they're awful. They are all about being submissive—what make-up, what clothes, how to kiss . . . all to please the boyfriend." She explains she has worked through a pile from the newsagent's to prepare for her girls' assertiveness group today.

Brian continues producing paper about the project, about Save the Children Fund's children's rights approach, about profiles of kids the project has taken on and worked with—submissiveness and injustice seems to figure large. A fair start appears not to be in it for many of the project's users.

Killearn Street

employment

In contrast to all of the kids I interview, who without exception consider Possilpark to be a dump, every grown-up I speak to about conditions in the area—local residents, community workers, police, professionals—want to stress the positives. Not that anybody wants to gloss over the problems—they just don't want all the good things, all the good people ignored.

Possilpark, which for the Befriending Project's purposes includes part of Ruchill, Lambhill, High Possil and the Milton, is the area of Glasgow bounded by Springburn to the east and Maryhill to the west. To the north the Balmore Road goes through open countryside to the prosperous suburb of Milngavie. To the south, and less than ten minutes by bus, is the city centre's main commercial and shopping area.

"This often forgotten part of the city," writes John O'Neill, depute Chief Executive of the enterprise and development agency Glasgow North Ltd, "has unemployment of around 6000 (in resident population of 76,000), with 50% having been out of work for over 12 months."

Contd. Page 24

forgotten part of the city—
looking from Hamilton Hill to Possil

20

Norman

Norman, at first sight, is the living opposite of the
demonised inner city/housing scheme teenage
male. Where the mythical demon youth is loud,
Norman is quiet. His very moving into the room is
soft and contained. The monster yobo youth is
chaotic in manner and appearance. Norman
arrives thirty minutes before the arranged time and
sits chatting softly to Glynis, the project's admin
secretary. He looks like an amiable young man.
His hair is light brown, medium length. He is
tallish, tidily if poorly dressed. His eyes hold mine
and tell of a pain beyond his 19 years.

"I had befrienders from the time I was
about . . . oh . . . 13, I think, till I was 18," he
explains in the same soft, almost languid tone. He
recounts them by name. "Doreen—she moved
away; then Julien until he moved to London. And
Kim." He still sees Kim sometimes. Even though

he's off the befriending scheme now, he goes to her house if she's not busy. "I just phone her."

"I saw her once a week, every week for 2 years. I went to her house, had a meal. I got on well with her husband, Robert." Kim and Robert at one stage offered him supported lodgings in their house, but Norman "had second thoughts."

"Befriending," he says, "has helped me cope with my problems. It took my mind away from them."

So what were Norman's problems? How come he first got on the scheme? "I never went to school," he says. Further quizzing and that's what it feels like, draws out Norman's criminal past—"I was caught on a train without a ticket." Pressing from Brian Wright extracts, "Oh, I was lifted, accused of being a look-out for somebody stealing a car."

Norman is circumspect. I ask him about his family. "I didn't go to school or go out because I wanted to make sure my ma was all right." He

won't expand. But he tells me he never knew his own dad. I leave him his privacy.

Later, and I'm not sure if Brian Wright is being specific, we talk about drink and domestic violence and kids feeling responsibility beyond their years.

This quiet unassuming young man—the kind you could easily imagine being pushed into standing look-out for wilder spirits, now lives in a council flat in neighbouring Maryhill. He tells me he's been on two Youth Training Schemes—for 5 months in shops, and for 15 months in catering. He's not worked since then.

An hour has passed. Another one would pass like this if it were up to Norman—"I visit the hostel I used to live in and I visit my mum," he replies when I ask him how he spends his time. "Sometimes I just go outside." And then he adds, "I don't think I'd go out as much if I hadn't been on this."

"Youth unemployment," he adds, at around 30% and rising, "is alarmingly high." He is writing in a paper of July 1993 on the Glasgow North Urban Programme Strategy. John O'Neill takes care to talk up the area's assets—"an indigenous employer base, easy transport access, M8 and M80 form our southern and eastern boundaries . . ." Rail links, 2 airports within 45 minutes, 2 Further Education colleges and 3 universities within walking distance . . .

Such undoubted assets in the spheres of industrial and commercial development do have the drawback of highlighting the social contrasts. Possilpark, Springburn and Maryhill may be easy to get to. For young unemployed people with a sense of dislocation and stunted hopes, they make it east to get out—"up the town" to shops and entertainments many of them can barely afford.

Given the figures in the school year 1991/92 for the area, not many of them are likely to achieve labour market status through educational attainment. Whereas in Strathclyde Region as a whole, 38% of young people leaving school in 1992 achieved 5 or

Contd. Page 30

majorettes at the after school club—
in 1992, 1% of the year group in
Glasgow North schools reached
University entrance level

Danny

Danny is 16. He expects to shake hands as we meet . . . firmly! He has sweat on his brow and is breathing a bit heavily. He's just been meeting his befriender, Rachel, and came here to the project office on his bike, at speed.

"Social work introduced me to this last year." Why? "I was on home supervision from the Panel." Why? "I wouldn't go to school. There were problems at home. I couldn't stay with my dad. We couldn't agree on anything, just fighting every day. I got fed up and went to Social work myself." He was 13 then. "I stayed in a children's home in Airdrie. I've been in about six homes since then but it doesn't work out when I go back.

"My dad thinks everyone has to do things his way—like coming in on time." He explains that his 2 older brothers and older sister have left home. His mother left the family home when he was 5.

27

"I used to hang about with 15 or 20 people and create havoc. Befriending's helped me. I can go out now and not get into bother. Rachel's nothing like a social worker—especially my social worker. You can say things to Rachel, talk about real things outside, like buzzing gas and things, things I wouldn't tell a social worker. It's like talking to one of your pals. The social worker would tell me to come to his office and give me a big mad lecture—Oh, I'll need to tell your mum and dad—sort of thing.

"It's the same with teachers—they would tell me what to do just like my dad. I can't stand people telling me what to do. Rachel will just sit and listen. Rachel treats me like a human being. A social worker gets paid for telling you things. Rachel tells me because she wants to tell me.

"My dad wouldn't even sit down and talk to me about anything—maybe I wouldn't listen even if he did sit me down—but he goes mental, hitting me, throwing things about."

28

All this has come out to me, a complete stranger, with only minimum prompting. Danny is angry. He is consumed by injustice. So clear is he about his own feelings that he imparts to me the sense that I am in the presence of a survivor. What, I wonder, would he want life to be like for himself when he's 30?

"I won't be like my dad," he throws back instantly. "I'll make sure that if I have weans of my own, they'll be able to come up to me and talk. I had nobody to talk to. One of the reasons I got into trouble was I never had anybody to talk to in my house."

Danny is doing a one year Community Service Volunteer placement as an after-school care play supervisor. He enjoys it—"it's good!" The job takes him out away from his dad. He had supported lodgings arranged through Social Work but it didn't work out. "Anything organised by a social worker falls to bits, by the way." He is not even half joking.

29

more Standard Grades, the figure for Glasgow North was 8%.

More dramatically, if higher education is the means to advancement, young people in Possilpark and neighbouring areas are staying put. In 1992, 1% of the year group achieved 5 Higher passes or more. That is 10 (ten) students got the necessary qualifications for university or degree level college courses.

Putting these figures to various people evoked no surprise. Many expect that from this year on, since the unpopular and much-opposed closure of Possilpark secondary school in 1992, educational attainment is likely to be even worse. In a world where territorial rights are high in the consciousness of the young, the feeling is that kids are just not travelling to their new school and truancy is "through the roof".

"You would have to praise people locally for the initiatives taken," says Alistair Murison. He is the Area Officer for Strathclyde's Community Education Department. I am listening, in his office in Rosevale Primary School in Scalpay Street in the Milton scheme, to Mr Murison talking up the area. Community efforts are prodigious—transport schemes, elderly forums, the enterprise group, there's a residential barge project . . . and other things, all made possible through the efforts of local people with help from Strathclyde Social Work and Education departments and voluntary organisations.

Housing tenure, he explains is almost wholly public sector but, again through local efforts in the housing association movement, type of tenure is slowly diversifying. As a community educationist, he is all too aware of traditions of trade union and other collective action in the area. Even ten years ago, after all, there was still an industrial base.

The Regional Council run 4 Community Education centres within the immediate area of Possilpark, Milton and Sighthill. Their main focus of work is on adult education and youth services. The £66k budget this year supports 12 statutory youth clubs or organised activity groups and Community Education supports a whole string of voluntary clubs and initiatives—through staffing, advice and helping young people to key into other resources.

Leaving aside doubts about the £66,000 budget spread around a community of 76,000 people, all of this sounds impressive and if the discussion with Alistair Murison were to stop at this point, Possilpark would be talked up to the greatest place in Glasgow. But what, I ask, is it really like growing up here?

He pauses. Then he says a little slowly, "Poverty and unemployment have to be major features." And then he adds, "and low educational achievement." And then after some further talk, "drugs".

"Possilpark is known in the city for drug abuse, a place where drug abuse is frequent. There are some recovery projects but the availability of drugs in the area to young people is so easy."

He seems moved by his own anecdote about how drug abuse and the economic pressure to be involved in associated shoplifting and criminal activities permeates the whole fabric of local society. "In our after-school service, we are all too aware of drug problems in families. Even little kids know all about drugs. When they play, they take on roles from parents going out to get drugs. Knowledge of drug abuse is high in the area."

"People want jobs, shopping, better housing, environmental improvements. We are constantly told by kids there's nothing to do. Not because there's nothing to do. It's just that in the scheme of things, going to a youth club, it's not seen as where it's at. These kids live 10 minutes in the bus away from the city centre and all the attractions of what life is supposed to offer.

"I think *there's nothing to do* is more about an apathy and an alienation, a feeling that what's available isn't good enough. The challenge for a youth worker here is to get young people actually participating, getting a sense of ownership of and valuing what they can do."

Contd. Page 38

good neighbours, Keppoch

gable wall mural, Saracen Cross—
an industrial past

Katrina

Katrina is 16 and had a befriender (Tracy) for a year either side of her 14th birthday. She tells me right off that she was under social work supervision and the social worker and her mum "put a stop to" the befriending.

"I saw Tracy afterwards a few times. But my mum was hitting the roof if I'd seen Tracy behind her back. I think I got too involved with my befriender—I treated her like a mother. I was seeing her 3 or 4 times a week. I couldn't speak to anyone, so I just got involved with Tracy and I was getting rebellious with my mum. Tracy came up one night and she and my mum had a big argument."

Confused? We have to run all that again. Katrina had started running away from home and just staying out at nights around the time when her older sister came back from living with their own

35

dad. He's been married 4 times. "She left the house and I left with her." Robert (her stepdad) really hated her for upsetting her mum.

"I went to a Panel," Katrina takes up the story, "got put in care for 6 months. I travelled in to school every day and got on well and my mum got really proud of me. It really helped me—the home was strict. I was quite ashamed of myself actually—I think I grew up a bit. I looked at things from their point of view."

"At the time, I couldn't really speak to my mum. I couldn't even mention about my sister. Tracy was nice to me. I could tell her things I couldn't tell my mother. But then I was telling her things that she couldn't keep to herself—so that was bad as well—like about boys and everything." Katrina, sitting somewhat demurely, tastefully and attractively made up, reminisces over an incident about shaved eyebrows. And then a long grotesquerie—an episode with overage boys up a close, being arrested and taken for a vaginal

examination by the police surgeon—result
negative, proven to be a virgin! So it was OK.

"Friendship was what Tracy could give me."
Katrina is working in a chippie and looks the part
to take up the college course in hairdressing that
she's applied for.

In the current popular demonology of inner-city or peripheral estate youth, crime—stealing cars, breaking into decent folks' houses, assembling in riotous mobs, public drunkenness—generally being misspent is the game.

I contact the Saracen Police Station in Barloch Street. Can I speak to someone about police perceptions of young people in the area? I am put through to Sergeant David Saunders in the Community Involvement Branch. I'd like to talk about what it's like for young people growing up in Possilpark.

"I can give you that in one word," the voice comes back, "dire!"

Can I come in and talk to you about it? "Sure. We're the low flat building in Barloch Street that looks like a bomb shelter."

Such honesty. I actually start looking forward to the meeting.

Sergeant David Saunders and Constable Jerry Docherty turn out to be realists with heart. Having already had earfuls of "never trust the polis" stories—

Contd. Page 44

policing

a policeman's lot—
Saracen station window

high-rise flats, Garscube

Karen and Linda

Karen and Linda are sisters. They bundle into the room. Karen's well-dressed in blouson jacket. She wears suede desert boots. Her fair hair is tied back from her face, showing bright eyes, full of life. Linda seems less outgoing. She's wearing a black bomber jacket and looks more withdrawn—just slightly, because they both banter their way through the discussion.

The gist of the story that bubbles out of them is that 6 years ago they came on the befriending scheme. Karen's now 20; Linda 18. They were both bad school attenders and both had been in care.

"I was doing a lot of stealing," says Karen. She speaks confidently but with a pronounced stutter. "And I was staying out at nights."

"Get the facts right, Karen," Linda interjects. "You used to drink and screw!" They both laugh.

Karen tells me they both "fell pregnant" around the same time nearly three years ago.

Home life seems to have verged on the chaotic. "I suppose some of it was my fault," says Karen. "But my mum and I just couldn't get on. With my mum and dad it was like having a cat and dog in the same room—hitting and fighting all the time." And then she adds by way of compensation, "I know my mum and dad loved us and that, but . . ."

"You started getting interested in boys and they were drinking so you drank—I wouldn't blame it all on my ma and da. It was Lesley (befriender) that helped me all the way. If it wasn't for her . . . I wouldn't be doing what I'm doing today." Karen seems pleased with her life. She got married to her boyfriend, her child's father, two months ago and she works in a fast food place.

She's doing the talking for both of them. Linda's eyes are brighter now, with admiration for her sister. Karen is explaining how she and Lesley used to go to the pictures, go for meals, go ice skating,

go back to Lesley's house—and Linda and her
befriender, Alison would join them.

"You'd do things you'd never done before,"
Linda chips in. "Like once we went to the circus."

"They took us to meet their families. It was like
having a good pal—but they weren't trying to get
you intae trouble. They would try to get you out o'
trouble. They were like sisters—you could tell them
things. Lesley had a lot of sense—she gave me
good advice—she told me to give up this boy."

If your mum had given you the same advice?
"I'd have told her to shove it!"

Linda says more than a little wistfully that after
Alison left, she was taken into a residential school
where she lived for 18 months.

Who's looking after the kids today? "My mum's
looking after mine," quips Karen in a
demonstration of humorous irresponsibility. Her
eyes catch mine and they say—I know I'm being
irresponsible. "I'm going back to work—another
day of freedom!"

"so long as they make an arrest, they don't care who", "help the polis, beat yourself up"—these officers come across as fair-minded, level-headed sociologists. Not for the first time on this assignment, I am crossing back and forth over the barriers of the divided society. Both sides in a war, when you listen to them, have got a point.

Without delving into all the figures, the picture that comes out about law-breaking and the young in Possilpark is one of cars and drugs. 80% of car crime—theft, joyriding, breaking into cars, road traffic offences—involve juveniles. If someone absconds from residential school, then you can see a blip upwards in car crime. Fatalities and near things are commonplace with kids driving stolen cars. "You can virtually guarantee a car chase somewhere in the Division every day," says Jerry.

In the part of Strathclyde Police C Division that comprises Possilpark, Ruchill and Milton, figures for 1992 show that 638 motor vehicles were reported stolen—a dozen a week. Bad enough. In the same year though a further 788 motor vehicles, stolen outwith the area were recovered here. Fifteen a week. A net trade surplus of a kind for Possilpark!

Drugs, "as everyone knows in the city," are a big problem in Possilpark. How do they know? While they look at me as if I've just landed from Mars, they list the evidence. Open dealing on the streets; high usage of rehab programmes; the number of arrests for drug offences—possession, possession with intent to supply; obstruction; a high proportion of crime related to feeding a habit. Heroin, temgesic and temazepam are the major features, mainly heroin. "Possilpark is a kind of drug trade area," explains Jerry. "Users come in from different parts of the city to get their supply. I mean," he adds as if to finally damn my apparent innocence, "why else would you get a queue of black taxis in some nondescript side street?"

Wise up. I give out signals that I too have read the papers and Possilpark's drug reputation goes before it. I just can't make up about it. They are reassured. Not for the first time, people are articulating feelings about the conditions that prevail as a matter of course. There is a latent anger that life should be like this.

Saunders and Docherty loosen up. These big policemen show a level of empathy with Possilpark people—thieves, joyriders, housebreakers, dealers, crooks—that would surely confound a Conservative Party conference law n'order audience.

"I've worked in some bad areas in my time," says David Saunders shaking his head, "but the deprivation here is the worst I've ever seen. Sure there have been environmental improvements in pockets where the housing associations have taken over, but the standard of housing is terrible.

"Wee tots have been brought up to accept things as normal—talk about drugs, squalor." He digs out a photograph of one of the school groups who come on visits to the police station. "This is a good example of what it's like for kids here. I mean, we're showing them round, looking at posters and things. Most of them, even 8 and 9 year olds, can hardly read the information." He points to a "lovely wee girl", one of several in the group photo taken in the station, who are kitted out in school uniform. "She says, ah think ma brother's been in here. How's that, I ask her. Oh, she says, the drugs squad put him in a van."

"My own personal view is that a lot of effort is put in here to help people in various ways. But when it comes down to it, the big problem is there's no jobs. People have no prospects. What ambition can you have? So they just have to get the most they can out of the system and sometimes that means crime."

We have drifted—is this a surprise?—into the tired old, but oh so contemporary question: crime and poverty, is there a connection? These two declare the usual arguments—just because you're unemployed, you're not a bad person; every jobless person doesn't get into doing drugs. But at the end of the day—they cite the problems of 16-18 year olds

Contd. Page 54

—into cars　　　let's get—

found in the
scrapyard

Possilpark secondary school—
now closed

Benny and Sammy

Benny and Sammy are both 15. They've come together and that's the way they seem to prefer to talk about their experience of befriending. Benny is the taller of the two and the more talkative. His eyes are more alert and hold contact better than Sammy's. The discussion is lively and stilted in turn. But first it's lively.

They're telling me about their befrienders. "Robert's a great guy," says Benny. "He's a scaffolder—he lives in Possil, just up there." He points up the street. "It's great meeting Robert's pals anaw—they talk about all different things." He tells me they go to the pictures. They go skating and to Macdonalds. They have a good laugh. Every Thursday. They're going to the Scottish Motor Show tonight. Benny likes cars.

Sammy chips in about his trips out with Steve. It's competitive—who gets what, how much and

how often. Motor Show nothing—Sammy goes to the Laserquest with Steve every Thursday. And then as if to clinch victory in the affection stakes, Sammy shows the bill—"it costs him £2.50 for 5 minutes."

When I ask Sammy about his volunteer, he replies quietly that he's only been seeing Steve for a couple of months. Before that it was Linda for 2 years. "But she done a bunk—she just didnae turn up. She bolted." Then he adds obliquely, "just like another person that bolted." But he won't be drawn on this. He feels let down, abandoned even by his previous volunteer.

Benny is happy to talk about his circumstances when he came on the befriending scheme. He had been in care from age 12. His social worker, he explained, thought it a good idea to keep him out of the area once a week.

"I used to break into cars and things like that. So I went to Panels—lots of them. I was breaking

into cash & carry, theft, trespass, not going to
school, out of parental control . . ." His 'grounds
of referral' seem firmly imprinted on his memory. "I
never got caught though," he boasts.

Sammy can't resist the challenge and is eager
to fill in similar details from a wild past, some of it
shared with Benny.

"The whole o' Possil was efter him," jokes
Benny, part impressed, part putting down. They
seem to agree that so mental was Sammy's local
housebreaking and car stealing habits that he was
not a popular lad in the district. I pursue the
question as to what Sammy's family situation is.
He tells me he lives with his dad and 2 older
brothers, but he won't tell me what that's like. "I
don't want to tell him," he says to Brian Wright.
"There's already been a wee misunderstanding. I
just want to stay out of trouble."

"Do you want me to leave the room?" asks
Brian.

"No."

Benny gets back into gear again talking about himself. "Life couldn't be better." He works a milk round from 4 a.m. It's great speaking to lassies when they're going to school." He has a pride in his appearance and is interested in girls and appears interested in life. Sammy has slipped further down in his chair and is now yawning profusely.

Benny is reflecting that you feel guilty (for the thieving and things) but at the time you enjoy it. "The thing is, there's nothing for us tae dae here. They're not even goin tae open up that wee youth club. Young folk now," he says, "they get intae drugs an that. You see young boys now—12, 13—jumping aboot the streets steamin."

Benny expresses the strong opinion that kids in schemes like Easterhouse and Castlemilk have got better facilities—swimming pools, clubs and things—than them in Possil. He condemns the work experience organised by school as rubbish. He's

out of trouble and his ambition is to get a real job.
He does his milk round, goes to school, he sees his
mates, he's interested in girls, and he does
weights.

"I can never think of anythin tae dae," yawns
Sammy.

who can't get benefits because they've to do training schemes that aren't always available—it's kind of obvious.

The station Prisoner Documentation—the lock-up book—at Saracen shows the age profile of offending. Of the 353 individuals detained during the months of July, August, September and October 1993, 15% were juveniles (age 16 or under). It's a safe assumption, I am told, that most of the rest would be in the 16-22 age band.

Stealing cars and injecting heroin seem like two shades of the same response. If life in Possilpark, notwithstanding the brave efforts of many residents to improve things, is typified by high unemployment, bad housing, poor amenities, family breakdown, acute feelings of relative deprivation, social dislocation and hopelessness, revving up a stolen car is one way of simulating control. Shooting up drugs is another. They could represent quite neatly the manic and the depressive sides of responding to life's stress.

Contd. Page 60

public gaze

notice

Tricia

Tricia is 16. Within 3 minutes of meeting her, she puts the effect of befriending bluntly.

"If Sheila wasn't here, I might not be here!" Sheila, a student nurse who's just finishing her degree, has come along to this interview with her. The power of Tricia's words produces a momentary silence.

I check it out. Yes, she feels she might be dead. Befriending could have saved her life, literally. "Having someone to talk to," says Tricia who seems a shy quiet-spoken young woman, "it's important."

Tricia was being bullied at school so she was not attending. She was being bullied in the street as well. Her mum and dad were rowing at home and as the eldest of 4 daughters, she and her mum were rowing. She has been suicidal. No one to talk to. The social worker was really for her mum—

"she didn't have time to listen to me. She would rush me."

"I never realised the extent of Tricia's problem, to be honest," says Sheila when I ask her about her lifesaving contribution. "I just enjoy being with her, going out." They go bowling and things. Sheila finishes her course next week. "I might be suicidal as well," she laughs. A degree for unemployment! Tricia laughs too, a big broad smile.

They laugh again when they recall the story about how Tricia got the job she does in a chip shop. Sheila had gone with Tricia to the Careers Office which had been a bit of an ordeal. Then coming back there was a SITUATION VACANT notice in a chip shop window. Sheila told me after much hanging about, she just "pushed her in the door".

"And I got it!" said Tricia, as if still incredulous.

I try to get a picture of the source of Tricia's despair. I press her on her relationship with her

mother. What does she think the rows are about really? Her sisters?

"I'd rather not say about home," she says eventually. She's told me enough. And she's given me the feeling that she knows much more than she's saying. She's not without insight either. "We blame each other. My ma realises she shouts at me, but . . ."

She has her name down on the housing list. Her future would be "a decent job, a wee hoose, a better life." She doesn't want any kids.

Questions to people about political initiatives generate incredulity, consternation and contempt in equal measure. "I don't vote because of the Poll Tax." "I couldn't care about politics, to be honest." In regard to the city council—"They do fuck all for us up here." One man amplified the theme as he reflected on the fact that, come to think of it, you didn't even hear from them during elections now. His eyes showed a fondness for the days when parties would go round the schemes announcing their message through an indecipherable loudspeaker—now alas, even that small trace of contact with official power, no more!

In the parlance of political pundits, like most of west central Scotland which contains half of the country's population, Possilpark is a "Labour fiefdom". Among the Labour representatives on Strathclyde Regional Council, local councillor Gerald McGrath is deputy leader. The representative on Glasgow City Council is John Innes, the city's provost. (Since this was written, Mr. Innes has died.) Two parliamentary constituencies dissect the area. They are held by Labour MPs Maria Fyfe and Michael Martin.

A fiefdom? Strangely, no one I spoke to was a member of the Labour Party, no-one knew where Party meetings were held. None of the local school or community centres, traditional meeting places, ever held branch meetings. "They don't have a high profile locally," a professional put it to me.

One man, a local resident in Possilpark all his life, expressed it a bit more trenchantly. "Labour is just a tradition here. The thing is, it doesn't matter what people here say—you're walked over. People up here have not got the confidence. When they do act (he cited the Possilpark Secondary School campaign against closure), it just gets slapped back in their face." He had no love for the council, the Labour Party, or government at all for that matter. He doesn't vote "because of the Poll Tax."

Brian Wright hands me a sheet of paper—"some figures we did, trying to make a profile of the kind of kids we get referred here." Of 58 referred as possibly suitable for befriending last year, the "categories of problem" are everything, after a walk around Possilpark, that you might expect.

43 were listed as having family problems; 16 specified health problems—their own or in the family; 20 were experiencing drug or alcohol problems. Domestic violence, physical, sexual or emotional abuse, and school problems of one type or another—special needs, bullying, truancy—were the predominant features. Almost a third of this referred group were subject to statutory supervision by a social worker. A number of referrals were isolated or profoundly uncommunicative in some way.

So what happened when I arranged to see a sample of these young people from Possilpark who made up these, by any standards, disturbing profiles? Of the 10 contacts made with a group of kids from family and personal circumstances ranging from the chaotic, the alcoholic, the addicted, the poor and the disconnected, 9 turned up. All of them on time, all communicative. Some were still seeing befrienders; most had finished their time on the scheme. All were in large measure appreciative of what they had gained. One young woman felt, if it were not for her befriender, having made several suicide attempts before, chances are she wouldn't be here now. For most, their befrienders were felt to be a pivotal relationship in their development. Several led me to form the impression that in talking about their time on the project, they were grieving the end of a valued experience.

The tenth contact? It was me that cancelled. A young man in a residential school—something to do with involvement in drugs, people after him in the area, the befriending is about planning ahead to the day when he can return home with some alternative community supports. A good story, but I felt intrusive with it.

Contd. Page 70

making friends

liven up

take that

Jimmy

Jimmy is 17. He's doing an HND course in computing at a city Further Education college. He did well at school—4 Highers in English, Computing, Physics and Chemistry and 7 Standard Grades. "Not good enough to get intae university, but."

He tells me he's been on Social Work supervision for the last 7 years. He doesn't know his dad—wouldn't recognise him on the street—and has lived with his aunt, separate from his mum and 4 brothers since he was 10. "My aunt told me my mum wanted me to stay with her so I could get out of the children's home."

Why had he been taken into care? Jimmy describes himself as having been "a bit of a tearaway". He had "behavioural difficulties" at primary school. He had trouble at home but he can't remember what that was. His social worker

65

put him forward for befriending.

His befriender is Rhona. He's been seeing her for a few months. She's a student at the university. He thinks she's in her twenties. They go to the cinema.

"I'm meeting a lot of different people through Rhona. Like students, people from different parts of the world, people with different attitudes. I treat Rhona more as a friend than a social worker." Jimmy has recently moved out of his aunt's and is now staying in digs with a landlady arranged by Social Work.

"I don't make friends easily. Normally I stay in at weekends. I don't go to clubs or anything—I can't dance." He starts to get into talking abut himself. He first tells me a long story about computer games—he plays them a lot. I reflect on this tall, dark, good-looking young man living in a landlady's room in a council flat in Possil. I ask about people on his college course. Does he get on with people there?

"I find I can mould with people in college."
He's not exactly looking happy with the moulding
process. "I know I can be quite annoying," he
says, like a confession, without prompting. And
then expressing his greatest fear, "the way I'm
going just now, I'll die a lonely old man."

"I don't think I show any emotions. My gran
died and I couldn't say anything—I just felt empty.
My mum is very emotional."

I mention something about knowing your own
feelings and he tells me about a dream he has
recurringly. It's about things not being in their
place. This young man's feelings, I form the
impression, are not in any kind of order. He seems
to feel manipulated and controlled—"I still get
annoyed about people getting me to do things—
things I don't like doing. I try to be my own person
but there are problems that way."

One major problem seems to be that if it were
not for Rhona, he would have only acquaintances
not friends at college and his lonely room and

Commodore console at nights. We've been at this an hour, me a complete stranger. I'm going to see someone else. I feel he would happily spend the whole afternoon.

"My life in 10 years time?" he repeats the question. He hesitates after he states the obvious, good job, nice house. And then this intelligent lonely youth, all of whose significant adults— mother, aunt, dead gran, social worker, befriender—are women, says, "Maybe a nice wife but I'm not sure about relating to girls."

Lizzie (age 13) with befriender

Did the involvement in befriending show any lasting consequences? The young people interviewed speak for themselves. But one remarkable fact about the time spent researching and writing such an account bears a mention. Among associates in publishing, in business, writing and journalism, a common response to what I was doing was telling.

"Don't they find," went the gentle and discrete enquiry, "that some of the volunteers 'take advantage of' their position?" So accepting is the public at large of the exploitative, self-seeking nature of all relationships, the fear is that anybody who gives up their own time and energy to help someone else must be soft in the head or in it for their own (devious) motives.

The Befriending Project staff explained the exhaustive selection and training processes they run. Unlike most of the health, care and education jobs in the country where people have responsibility for children, these include police checks. "In six years," said Brian Wright holding the table, "we've had no disasters." As my gaze looks over his shoulder, out the window and over the rooftops of this stricken urban landscape towards the Campsie hills to the north of the city, the real disaster is in front of our eyes.

Lizzie (age 18) with son

In this the 75th year of Save the Children, the proprietor of Argyll Publishing was asked to evaluate their work in the befriending project in Glasgow's Possilpark.

The Possilpark housing scheme, barely 2 miles from the city's main commercial centre, presents young people with formidable obstacles to growing up.

Fair Start is the result of talking to people who live there—local residents, professionals, Save the Children staff and volunteers and the police. Most of all, **Fair Start** allows the young—the popularly demonised joyriders, housebreakers, teenage mothers, youth trainees, the unemployed and others—the chance to do what society usually denies them. To speak up for themselves.

The author, Derek Rodger, is a writer and publisher. He is widely experienced in children's and family matters, and is a former editor of *Scottish Child* magazine.